CULTURAL SITES

FOREIGN LANGUAGES PRESS

First Edition 2004

ISBN 7-119-03402-2
©Foreign Languages Press, Beijing, China, 2004
Published by Foreign Languages Press
24 Baiwanzhuang Road, Beijing 100037, China
Website: http://www.flp.com.cn
E-mail Addresses: Info@flp.com.cn
Sales@flp.com.cn
Distributed by China International Book Trading Corporation
35 Chegongzhuang Xilu, Beijing 100044, China
P.O. Box 399, Beijing, China

Printed in the People's Republic of China

Preface

As a world-renowned country with an ancient civilization, China boasts a wealth of cultural relics and historical sites, such as the ten thousand-li Great Wall, the Imperial Palace in Beijing, the Dunhuang Grottoes, and the Potala Palace in Lhasa. In particular, the Great Wall has been called one of the Wonders of the World.

It has become the common responsibility of all mankind to preserve the natural and cultural wealth created by our ancestors. Moreover, people are becoming more aware of the importance of looking after these priceless treasures so that we can hand them down to later generations. Over the past few decades, people throughout the world have made efforts to various degrees to preserve their cultural and natural heritages. In the third century BC, the Ramses Dynasty in Egypt established a mouseion, from which the English word "museum" is derived, in the imperial palace in Alexandria. It was a special temple for housing valuable cultural relics. The pyramids of Egypt and ancient structures of many other countries in the world have been preserved by the authorities. China boasts a collection of inscriptions on bones and tortoise shells which date from the Shang Dynasty (18th-11th centuries BC). In the Zhou Dynasty (C. 1100-221 BC), a great number of famous articles and valuables were kept in special collection rooms, and registered in the *Records*. Besides collecting valuable cultural relics, the local authorities in China throughout history made efforts to preserve special palaces, cemeteries and ancestral temples, mountains, rivers, trees, historical sites, gardens and ponds. There was also a solid folk tradition of preserving public buildings, ancestral temples and guild halls, irrigation works, mountains, rivers and trees through local rules and popular conventions. The details of such preservation measures were inscribed on tablets.

With the development of communications, information transmission and tourism, people have become more aware of the importance of protecting their cultural and natural heritages, especially from damage resulting from industrialization in the modern era. Therefore, some experts, scholars and far-sighted personages of various countries have made appeals for joint protection of the common wealth of mankind, and passed the Athens Charter, Venice Charter, Washington Charter, Lausanne Charter, the Europe and American conventions to preserve archaeological and historical heritages, the Suggestions on the Protection of the Landscape and the Styles, Features and Characteristics of Relics of the United Nations Educational, Scientific and Cultural Organization (UNESCO), etc. To further strengthen the protection and management of cultural relics, and get national governments to pay more attention and extend more support to these endeavors, the Convention on the Protection of the World's Cultural and Natural Heritages was adopted at the 17th UNESCO Conference in Paris in November 1972, explicitly regulating the definition and standards of the world's cultural and natural heritage sites, and setting the guiding principle of its implementation, which is a standard international document of far-reaching influence promulgated and carried out by UNESCO throughout the world. One of its main tasks is to determine items of cultural and natural heritage of prominent significance and universal value generally accepted by the whole world, and list them in the World Heritage List as the common heritage of mankind, to promote cooperation and mutual support among people of all countries and ethnic groups, and make active contributions to the protection of this heritage.

To guarantee that all the regulations of the Heritage Convention win the support and cooperation of all countries, the World Heritage Committee (WHC), an organization of international cooperation between governments was founded in 1976, supported by 21 of the signatory states to the Convention on the Protection of the World's Cultural and Natural Heritage. The organization's headquarters is the UNESCO Center for the Protection of the World Heritage. The WHC holds a meeting every year, to mainly engage in three items of work: First, discussing and determining the projects to be proposed for inclusion in the World Heritage List and submitting them to the representative conferences of the signatory states for adoption and promulgation. Second, supervising the World Heritage Fund, and examining and approving the financial and technical support put forward by the signatory states. The fund is composed of one percent of the regular membership dues of UNESCO member states and voluntary contributions from the governments of the signatory states and other organizations and individuals. Despite its small size, the fund has played an active role in promoting the protection of some important items of cultural and natural heritage in many countries, especially the developing countries and underdeveloped regions. Third, monitoring the protection and management of the cultural and natural heritage projects listed in the World Heritage List.

To improve the quality of the work of protection, evaluation, survey and technical support, UNESCO and the WHC consult the International Council on Monuments and Sites (ICOMOS), International Union for the Protection of Nature and Natural Resources (IUCN), and the International Center for the Study of the Preservation and Restoration of Cultural Property (ICCROM), which assist with research and publicity work, as well as offering the services of experts.

Definitions of cultural heritage:

1. Cultural relics: Viewed from the historic, artistic or scientific angle, the buildings, sculptures and paintings of prominent and universal value, components and structures of archaeological significance, inscriptions, caves, residential areas and various combinations of the above.

2. Buildings: Viewed from the historic, artistic or scientific angle, independent or associated buildings of prominent and universal value due to their style, structure or position in the landscape.

3. Ruins: Viewed from the historic, aesthetic, ethnological or anthropological angle, artificial projects or common masterpieces of man and nature, and archaeological ruins of prominent and universal value.

4

Evaluation standards for cultural heritage sites:

1. Masterwork representing a unique achievement or creative talent.

2. Work that has had a significant influence on the development of architecture, urban construction or landscape designs during some period or in some cultural region in the world.

3. Work that can offer a unique or at least special evidence for a lost civilization or cultural tradition.

4. Work that shows one or several important stages of human history as an example of the masterwork of a kind of building or landscape.

5. Vulnerable site as an example of the human residential area or usable land of one or more cultural traditions, especially if an irreversible change threatens.

6. Material object of special universal significance, directly or substantially associated with modern current traditional ideas, beliefs or literary or artistic works. (According to experts, this article can be considered as a standard for a cultural heritage site listed in the World Heritage List only under some special situation or when it is jointly considered with other standards.)

Definition of natural heritage:

1. Viewed from the aesthetic or scientific angle, geological or biological structures of prominent and universal value or the natural features of similar structures.

2. Viewed from the scientific or protection angle, geological or natural geographical features of prominent and universal value, and explicitly designated habitats of endangered species of animals and plants.

3. Viewed from the scientific or natural aesthetic angle, natural scenic spots of prominent and universal value, or explicitly designated nature reserves.

Evaluation standards for natural heritage sites:

1. Outstanding examples of the important stages of the history of global evolution.

2. Important phenomena occurring during the process of geological or biological evolution, and important examples of the relations between man and the natural environment.

3. Unique, rare or ingenious natural phenomena or topographic features, or locations of rare natural beauty.

4. Habitats of rare or endangered animals or plants.

In addition, the WHC may list seriously threatened or endangered sites of cultural and natural heritage in the World Heritage List so as to adopt emergency measures to save and protect them after investigations and discussions by experts.

Always attaching great importance to the protection of items of cultural and natural heritage, the government of the People's Republic of China actively takes part in activities designed to protect the world's cultural and natural heritages carried out by UNESCO and the CWH. In November 1985, at the proposal of relevant experts, scholars and members of the Chinese People's Political Consultative Conference (CPPCC), the Standing Committee of the National People's Congress gave China approval to become one of the signatory states to the Convention on the Protection of the World's Cultural and Natural Heritages of UNESCO. In 1986, China requested that the Great Wall, the Imperial Palace in Beijing, the relics of Peking Man at Zhoukoudian, the Mogao Grottoes at Dunhuang, the Mausoleum of the First Qin Emperor and the terracotta army and Mount Taishan be included in the World Heritages List. The request was approved by the WHC in 1987, after careful examinations. China was elected one of the members of the WHC at the Eighth Conference of the Signatory States to the Convention on the Protection of the World's Cultural and Natural Heritages in October 1991. China's representative was elected vice-president of the committee at the 16th and 17th conferences of the WHC in 1992 and December 1993, respectively.

The culture and traditions of the Chinese nation have had an unbroken history of several thousand years. As a country composed of many ethnic groups since ancient times, China has created a brilliant multi-ethnic culture in the process of its long historical development, represented by many masterpieces, such as the Potala Palace and the Chengde Mountain Resort and Its Outlying Temples. The murals and painted sculptures in the Mogao Caves at Dunhuang, and the Mausoleum of the First Qin Emperor and his terracotta army are also world-famous cultural treasures. In the realm of natural heritage, scenic areas such as those of Jiuzhaigou and Wulingyuan are characterized by unique geological and topographical features, animals and plants, and beautiful scenery. Many sites with both natural and cultural heritage features, including Taishan, Wuyi and Emei mountains, and the Leshan Giant Buddha Scenic Area, reflect the integration of China's long history and culture with its natural environment, which is rarely seen in other countries. Meanwhile, the cultural scenic spot of Mount Lushan has been approved for putting on the List as "an ingenious work integrating a beautiful natural environment with excellent human artistry."

As a contribution to protecting, studying and giving publicity to the world's cultural and artistic heritages, the Foreign Languages Press has produced this small album which introduces sites in China which have been recognized by UNESCO as being worthy of inclusion in its list of the common cultural and artistic wealth of mankind.

Luo Zhewen
Vice-President of China ICOMOS

China has a glorious ancient civilization and an enormous amount of precious material and non-material cultural sites that have survived until now and become the common treasure of all humanity. They include grand ancient projects, such as the world-famous Great Wall and the Dujiangyan Irrigation System near Mount Qingcheng; uniquely designed and well-preserved ancient towns and villages, such as the old town of Lijiang, the ancient city of Pingyao, and the ancient villages of Xidi and Hongcun; graceful and delicate classical gardens, such as those in Suzhou; cultural sites revered by Chinese people, such as the Temple and Cemetery of Confucius, and the Kong Family Mansion in Qufu; rare remains of primitive man, such as those at the Peking Man site at Zhoukoudian; and uniquely charming examples of non-material heritage, such as Kunqu opera and ancient Chinese *guqin* music. The relics and sites mentioned, including the two forms of non-material culture, are among the 10 cultural sites that the UNESCO World Heritage Committee had approved for inclusion in the World Heritage List by November 2003. Of all that world civilization has produced, these examples of cultural heritage stand out and have become symbols of ancient Chinese culture.

- ❶ The Great Wall
- ❷ Peking Man Site at Zhoukoudian
- ❸ Temple and Cemetery of Confucius, and the Kong Family Mansion
- ❹ Old Town of Lijiang
- ❺ Ancient City of Pingyao
- ❻ Classical Gardens of Suzhou
- ❼ Ancient Villages in Southern Anhui—Xidi and Hongcun
- ❽ Mount Qingcheng and the Dujiangyan Irrigation System
- ❾ Kunqu Opera
- ❿ Chinese *Guqin* Music

Contents

The Great Wall (UNESCO cultural heritage site since 1987)

The Great Wall, as reconstructed in the Ming Dynasty (1368-1644), is located in north China, starting from the Yalu River on the border with Korea. It then extends westward through the municipalities of Tianjin and Beijing, Hebei Province, the Inner Mongolia Autonomous Region, Shanxi Province, Ningxia Hui Autonomous Region and Gansu Province, finally reaching the Jiayu Pass, with a total length of over 5,000 km. The history of its construction covers more than 20 centuries, dating back to the Spring and Autumn and Warring States periods (770-221BC), and continuing through the Qin, Han, Northern Wei, Eastern Wei, Northern Qi, Northern Zhou, Sui, Liao, Jin and Ming dynasties to the 17th century. If the Great Wall were dismantled, a road 10 m wide and 35 cm thick could be built to circle the earth twice. The various difficulties of the terrain — mountain ridges, deserts, grasslands, sheer cliffs and rivers — that the builders of the Great Wall had to overcome make it one of the wonders of ancient construction feats.

The Great Wall at Badaling.

The Great Wall, mainly used as a defense bulwark in ancient China, is pierced with loopholes for archers, and there are watchtowers at close intervals, as well as beacon towers. Due to its great influence for a period of over 2,000

Map of the Great Wall.

years on China's politics, military struggles and diplomatic contacts, there are many historical records as well as legends and folk tales about the Great Wall.

In 221 BC, the first emperor of the Qin Dynasty unified China and ordered that all the defensive walls in the north of all the previously warring states be joined and extended.

The Temple to Mengjiangnü

It is said that, during the first Qin emperor's reign, Mengjiangnü's husband was recruited shortly after they were married to build the Great Wall and he died at the construction site. Mengjiangnü traveled 500 km to visit her husband, only to see his corpse. The grieving Mengjiangnü cried and cried until the Great Wall collapsed. People of later generations built the temple at the foot of the Great Wall to commemorate her. ▼

In ancient times, the Great Wall was mainly used for military defense.

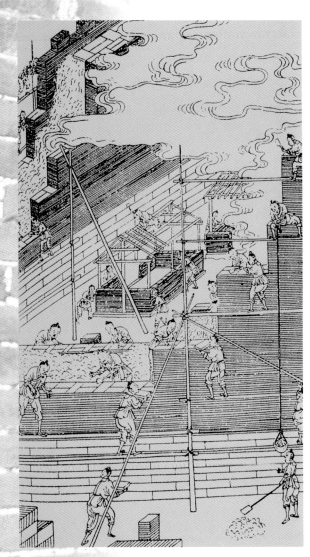

A picture of construction work on the Great Wall in the Ming Dynasty.

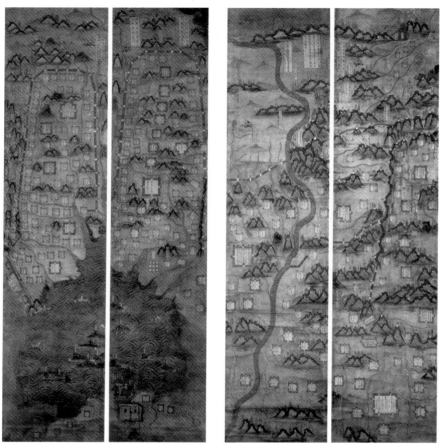

Large-scale construction on the Great Wall took place over the longest period during the Ming Dynasty. The silk scroll "Nine Frontiers" shows in detail the positions of the nine border towns along the Ming Dynasty Great Wall and the mountains and rivers around them.

The Jiayuguan Pass—the western end of the Great Wall in Gansu Province.

Walking on the Great Wall.

The morning sun seen through a watchtower on the Great Wall.

The Great Wall at Mutianyu in Beijing's northern suburbs.

Crenels on the Great Wall at Jinshanling in Hebei Province.

The Great Wall at Jiankou in Beijing's northern suburbs.

A moonlit Great Wall at Jinshanling in Hebei Province.

Peking Man Site at Zhoukoudian (UNESCO cultural heritage site since 1987)

This prehistoric site, at the northern foot of Mount Longgu in the Fangshan District, southwest of Beijing City, was first excavated in 1921. Peking Man lived 700,000-230,000 years ago. The fossils of three human teeth were unearthed from the Peking Man caves in 1921, 1923 and 1927, respectively, and a skull, stone tools and traces of fire were discovered there in 1929.

Excavation of the first site in 1921.

Excavation of the first site in 1935.

The main members of the Peking Man excavation team in 1934 (left to right): Pei Wenzhong, Li Siguang, Pierre Teilhard de Chardin, Bian Meinian, Yang Zhongjian and George B. Barbour.

The third site, discovered in 1927, where the fossils of 56 mammal species from the late Middle Pleistocene Epoch were excavated.

A model of Peking Man's head.

A cave where the Peking Man lived.

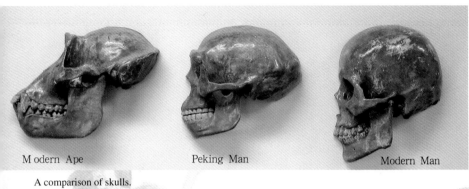

Modern Ape   Peking Man   Modern Man

A comparison of skulls.

1929年北京猿人第一头盖骨发现处

The first skull-cap of Peking Man was discovered here in 1929

A section of accumulation at the Peking Man caves.

Temple and Cemetery of Confucius, and the Kong Family Mansion (UNESCO cultural heritage site since 1994)

Confucius (551-419 BC), whose family name was Kong, was one of China's greatest thinkers and teachers. His residence, located in Qufu, Shandong Province, was converted to the Confucius Temple the year after his death for the holding of annual sacrifices to his spirit. Confucian doctrine became the state ideology throughout most of China's feudal dynasties, and as a result the scale of the Confucius Temple was constantly expanded, until now it has an area

of 327.5 mu (22 ha.) and 466 buildings. The temple grounds house a number of steles bearing relief carvings and inscriptions, which are valuable materials for studying ancient Chinese calligraphy, culture and art.

The Kong Family Mansion, to the east of the Confucius Temple, contains a collection of precious historical records and cultural relics.

The 3,000-odd-mu cemetery is the Kong family cemetery. Confucius himself is buried there, alongside thousands of his descendants.

The Confucius Temple's Lingxing (Literate Star) Gate, the first entrance to the temple.

Dragon columns in front of the Dacheng
(Great Accomplishments) Hall.

A caisson ceiling of Xingtan (Apricot Altar) Pavilion.

Xingtan (Apricot Altar) Pavilion, where Confucius used to give lectures.

Confucius giving a lecture.

A Ming Dynasty portrait of Confucius preserved in the Kong Family Mansion.

The tomb of Confucius.

The Kong Family Mansion's Old Well on the east side of the Confucian Temple, and Lu Wall (named after the ancient state in today's Shandong Province).

The screen wall in the inner quarters of the Kong Family Mansion.

The main hall of the Kong Family Mansion.

A room in the Kong Family Mansion.

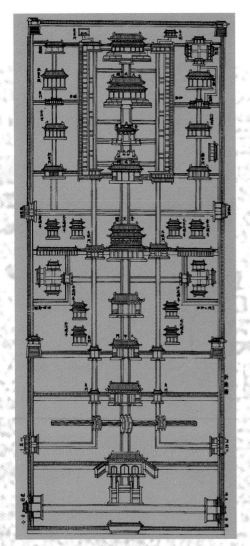

A map of the Confucius Temple drawn during the Ming Dynasty.

The palace wall around the Confucius Temple, built according to the imperial palace style.

The memorial arch leading to the Confucian Cemetery.

Old Town of Lijiang (UNESCO cultural heritage site since 1997)

The ancient city of Lijiang is located on a plateau 2,400 m above sea level, at the foot of Yulong (Jade Dragon) Snow Mountain in the Lijiang Naxi Autonomous Region of Yunnan Province. It dates from the end of the 12th century and has an area of 3.8 sq km. With neither the

regular road network nor city walls, the city has buildings in a unique combination of the architecture of the Central Plains and the traditional architectural styles of the Bai and Tibetan ethnic groups. A stream flows past every household. Important parts of the local cultural heritage are the Dongba religion and its peculiar script, and the Baisha Murals.

The first bend along the 10,000-li (5,000-km) Yangtze River.

Heilong (Black Dragon) Pool and Yulong (Jade Dragon) Snow Mountain.

A marketplace.

Small bridges over a stream.

A street corner.

An elderly Dongba shaman.

The written Dongba language of the Naxi ethnic group.

50

Elderly people in Sifang Street.

An elderly woman
sitting by a gate.

A performance of ancient Naxi music.

Ancient City of Pingyao (UNESCO cultural heritage site since 1997)

Pingyao is situated in Pingyao County, Shanxi Province. First built over 2,700 years ago, the ancient city has basically retained the historical features of the Ming (1368-1644) and Qing (1644-1911) dynasties in its more than 100 streets and lanes.

The Pingyao city wall.

Pingyao emerged as a center of finance in the mid-19th century, playing an important role in the development of the modern Chinese economy.

A map of the ancient city of Pingyao.

Wenshui County

Zhenguo Temple   Qixian County

Longfu Temple

Cixiang Temple

Yongfu Temple

Pingyao Ancient City

Jinzhuang Confucian Temple

Yin Family's Residence

Shuanglin Temple

Baifu Temple

Guo Family's Residence

Xigou Cliff Rock Carvings

Xiujie City

White Cloud Temple

Chaoshan Scenic Area

A tower over Mingqing Street in central Pingyao.

Zhenguo (Stablizing the Country) Temple.

Watchtowers.

Houses in the city of Pingyao.

Wood carvings.

58

Inside a Pingyao house.

An old bank.

Account documents from an old bank.

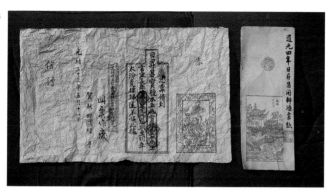

Statues of arhats in Shuanglin (Twin Groves)Temple.

Some of the 500 Bodhisattva statues in the Hall of a Thousand Buddhas. With their lifelike shapes and their colorful and diverse clothing and ornaments, they are valuable for the study of ancient Chinese life.

A statue of Skanda enshrined in Shuanglin Temple's Hall of a Thousand Buddhas.

Inside Shuanglin Temple's Bodhisattva Hall.

The Thousand-Hand Avalokitesvara, the main statue in the Bodhisattva Hall, symbolizes her omnipresence, omnipotence and infinite powers.

A narrow street in the city of Pingyao.

A brick carving on
a watchtower.

A gateway.

Liuyuan (Lingering) Garden.

Classical Gardens of Suzhou (UNESCO cultural heritage site since 1997)

Suzhou City in Jiangsu Province is famous for its classical gardens, the earliest of which was established in the sixth century BC. As the most prosperous region in China during the Ming and Qing dynasties, it has over 200 gardens dating from those times (16th-18th centuries), and dozens of them are still perfectly preserved.

Suzhou's classical gardens are integrated with residences and parks, created to bring the quiet of the countryside into the busy heart of the city. Typical of the classical private gardens are the Zhuozheng (Humble Administrator's) and Liuyuan (Lingering) gardens, and the Huanxiu Mountain Villa.

In December 2000, UNESCO listed the Canglang (Surging Waves) Pavilion, Shizilin (Lion Grove), Yipu (Art) Garden, Ouyuan (Couple's) Garden and Tuisi (Seclusion and Meditation) Garden as the five scenic spots of prominent value and universal significance among Suzhou's ancient gardens in the World Heritage List.

A lattice window in the Liuyuan (Lingering) Garden.

The Small Flying Rainbow in the Zhuozheng or Humble Administrator's Garden.

The Humble Administrator's Garden.

The waterside corridor in the Humble Administrator's Garden.

71

An exquisite, vivid relief brick carving of figures and open-work decorative carving in the Wangshi or Fisherman's Garden.

藻耀高翔

A gate decorated with brick carvings in the Fisherman's Garden.

The central area of the Fisherman's Garden.

The Fisherman's Garden.

Shizilin or the Lion Grove.

The entrance to Canglang (Surging Waves) Pavilion.

Ming (Bright) Hall.

The Tuisi (Seclusion and Meditation) Garden.

The eastern part of the Ouyuan or Couple's Garden.

The piled rocks in the west of the Couple's Garden.

Inside the Couple's Garden.

The Huanxiu (Embracing Beauty) Mountain Villa.

The interior decoration of a hall in a classical Suzhou garden.

Various shapes of lattice windows and gateways.

Ancient Villages in Southern Anhui—Xidi and Hongcun (UNESCO cultural heritage site since 2000)

Due to their well-preserved traditional features, the ancient dwellings of commoners in Xidi and Hongcun Village in Yixian County, Anhui Province, are the first such ordinary houses to be put on the World Heritage List. As representative Anhui-style buildings, there are over 440 intact residences dating from the Ming and Qing dynasties, characterized by neat and orderly layout, and exquisite structure and decoration.

With a history of nearly 1,000 years and an area of almost 13 ha, Xidi Village, characterized by careful landscaping, still retains perfectly the typical features of the ancient villages of the Ming and Qing dynasties. In Hongcun Village, established in 1131, stands the grand and elegant Chengzhi Hall. The hall is noted for its fine wood carvings.

A typical courtyard in a traditional Xidi Village residence.

The memorial arch at the Xidi Village entrance.

A paving-stone water channel in Xidi Village.

A partition decorated with a wood carving of historical figures in a Hongcun Village residence.

Wood carvings in a Xidi Village residence.

A pond in Hongcun Village.

The Nanhu Academy of Classical Learning in Hongcun Village.

Ancient houses in Hongcun Village.

Li Bing's motto about controlling water.

Mount Qingcheng and the Dujiangyan Irrigation System (UNESCO cultural heritage site since 2000)

Mount Qingcheng, located in the southwest of Dujiangyan City, Sichuan Province, is over 2,000 m above sea level. Adorned with ancient trees, it is regarded as one of the birthplaces of Taoism. At one time, there were more than 100 Taoist temples, and even today dozens remain intact. Two of them are of particular interest — the Tianshi (Grand Master's) Cave and the Shangqing (Superior Heaven) Palace.

The Dujiangyan Irrigation System, a huge water-conservancy project and triumph of hydrology, was built by the local prefect Li Bing in 227 BC, during the reign of Emperor Zhao of Qin. It is situated west of Dujiangyan City, Sichuan Province. The oldest water-conservancy project in China — a landmark in the history of Chinese scientific and technological development, it is also the oldest and only extant major water-conservancy project without a dam diversion in the world. The project used to bring a lot of farmland under irrigation, turning the West Sichuan Plain into a "land of abundance." It still performs this role today.

A map of the areas irrigated by the Dujiangyan irrigation system, showing Mount Longquan and the Minjiang and Tuojiang rivers.

The Two Kings Temple to Li Bing and his son at Dujiangyan.

Fulong (Dragon Subduing) Temple on
Mount Qingcheng.

Heavenly Master Zhang, the founder of Taoism, who is said to have taught scriptures on Mount Qingcheng.

"Qingcheng, the Greatest Mountain in the World."

A chain bridge over the Minjiang, a river that forms part of the Dujiangyan irrigation system.

大清光緒元年季夏中澣穀旦

遏灣截角

逢正抽心

署水利同知中州胡圴撰并書

Li Bing's motto about controlling water.

Cave of the Thunder God, a Kunqu opera play.

Kunqu Opera (UNESCO intangible heritage of humanity since 2003)

Originating in East China's Jiangsu Province, Kunqu opera was the type of opera that had the most writers and works during the Ming and Qing dynasties. It features a unique tune system, with each play consisting of a set of tunes adapted from the verse style of classical Chinese literature. There is an abundance of plays with elegant, flowery lyrics. The performance of Kunqu opera, a highly comprehensive art form, combines singing and dancing, with spoken parts and movement. The history of Kunqu opera's growth represents the development of Chinese opera as a whole. As Kunqu opera has had a direct influence on the formation and development of many opera styles including Peking opera, it has gained a reputation as the "ancestor of a hundred operas" in China.

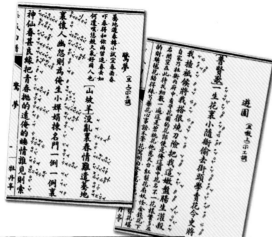

Wandering in the Garden, Waking from a Dream, a Kunqu opera play.

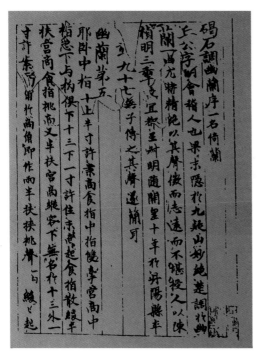

The score for a piece of *guqin* music.

Chinese *Guqin* Music (UNESCO intangible heritage of humanity since 2003)

Guqin music includes great achievements in Chinese instrumental music. The zither-like instrument is one of the world's earliest stringed musical instruments still extant, with a history of about 3,000 years. The art of the *guqin* consists of the manufacture of the instrument and its strings, the scores, music, history, songs, societies and schools. It has had a wide influence on China's musical, aesthetic, sociocultural and philosophical history. The *guqin* is a representative of ancient Chinese spiritual culture in music.

Boya, an ancient Chinese musician, plays the *guqin*.

A seven-stringed *guqin* from the Western
Han Dynasty (206 BC-25 AD).

A 10-stringed zither from around the time of Spring
and Autumn or Warring States periods (770-221 BC).

图书在版编目（CIP）数据

人文遗迹／罗哲文主编．－北京：外文出版社，2003.12
（中国的世界遗产）

ISBN 7–119–03402–2

Ⅰ.人...　Ⅱ.罗...　Ⅲ.名胜古迹－简介－中国－英文　Ⅳ. K928.7

中国版本图书馆 CIP 数据核字（2003）第 066634 号

策　　划	肖晓明
责任编辑	杨春燕
英文翻译	张韶宁
英文审定	郁　苓
图片提供	兰佩瑾　孙永学　孙志江　孙树明　刘春根
	杜泽泉　罗哲文　茹遂初　高明义　高纯瑞
版式设计	蔡　荣
印刷监制	张国祥

外文出版社网址：
　http://www.flp.com.cn
外文出版社电子信箱：
　info@flp.com.cn
　sales@flp.com.cn

中国的世界遗产

人文遗迹

罗哲文　主编

*

© 外文出版社
外文出版社出版
（中国北京百万庄大街 24 号）
邮政编码　100037
北京大容彩色印刷有限公司印制
中国国际图书贸易总公司发行
（中国北京车公庄西路 35 号）
北京邮政信箱第 399 号　邮政编码　100044
2004 年(小 24 开)第 1 版
2004 年第 1 版第 1 次印刷
（英）
ISBN 7–119–03402–2/J · 1657(外)
02800(平)
85–E–567 P